# TODAY'S POP HITS

## 2ND EDITION

ISBN 0-7935-3336-8

HAL•LEONARD®
CORPORATION

7777 W. BLUEMOUND RD. P.O. BOX 13819 MILWAUKEE, WI 53213

Visit Hal Leonard Online at
**www.halleonard.com**

# contents

# BEAUTIFUL

Words and Music by
LINDA PERRY

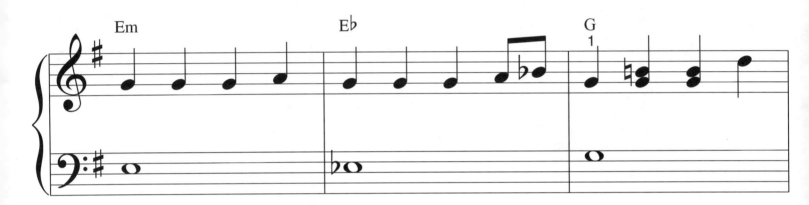

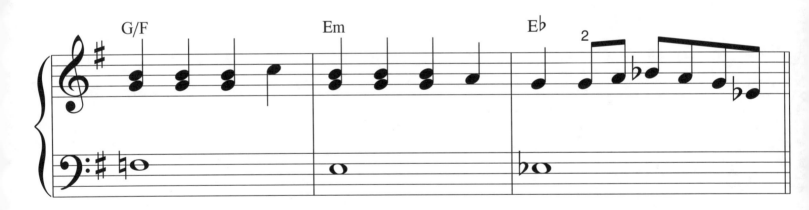

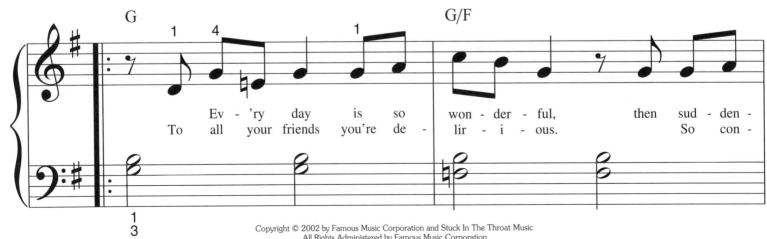

Ev - 'ry day is so won - der - ful, then sud - den -
To all your friends you're de - lir - i - ous. So con -

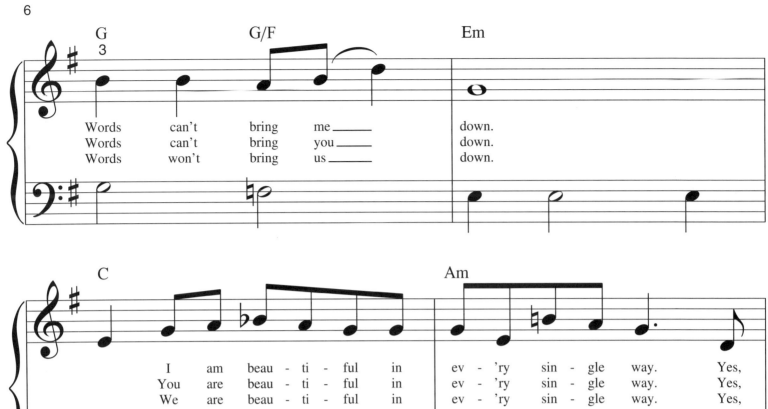

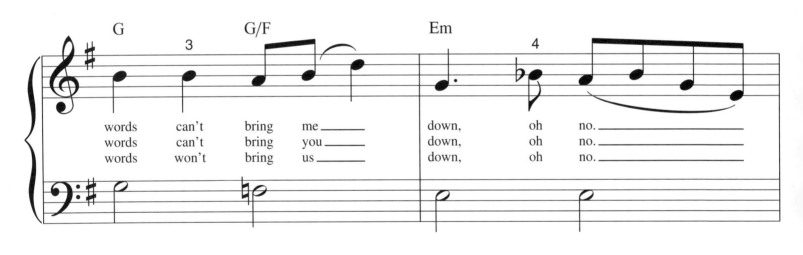

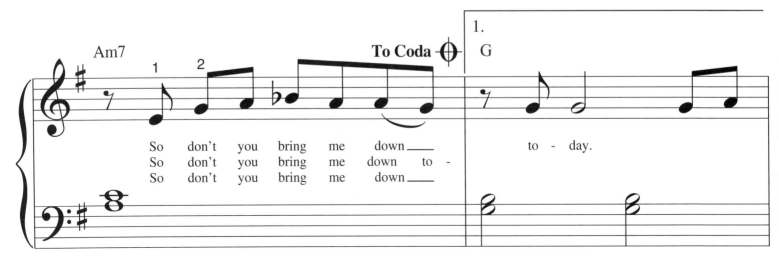

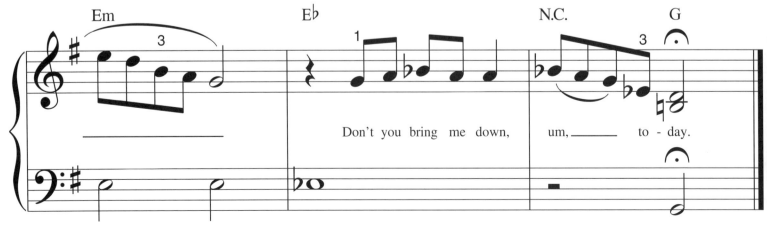

# COMPLICATED

Words and Music by AVRIL LAVIGNE, LAUREN CHRISTY,
SCOTT SPOCK and GRAHAM EDWARDS

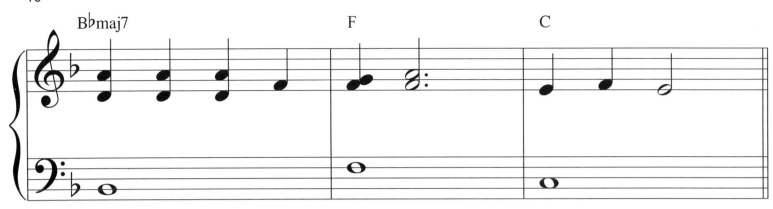

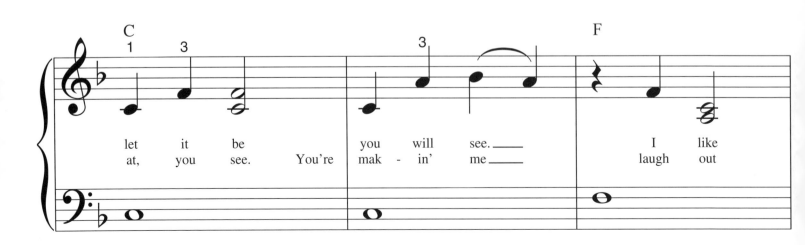

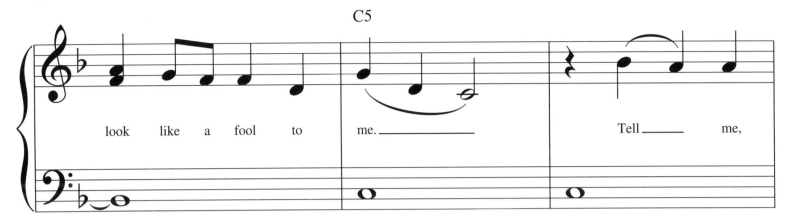

look like a fool to me._____ Tell_____ me,

why'd you have to go and make things so com - pli - cat - ed?

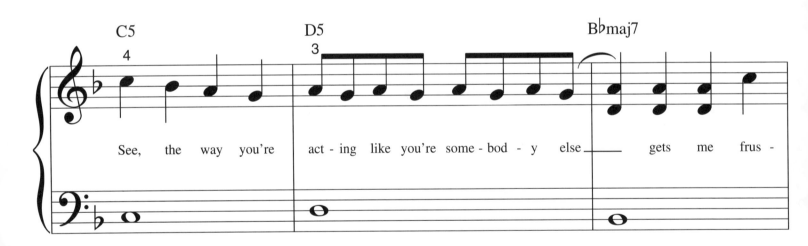

See, the way you're act - ing like you're some - bod - y else_____ gets me frus -

trat - ed. Life's like this, you, you fall and you

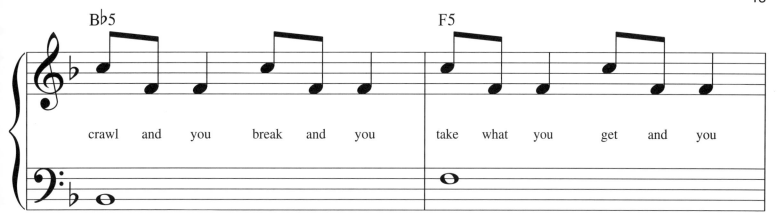

Bb5 — crawl and you break and you    F5 — take what you get and you

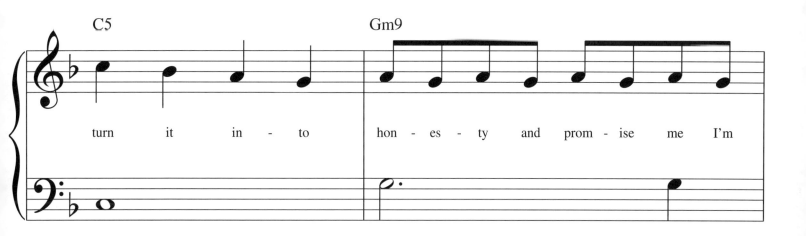

C5 — turn it in - to    Gm9 — hon - es - ty and prom - ise me I'm

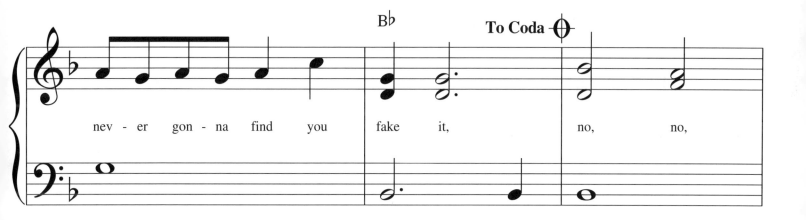

nev - er gon - na find you    Bb — fake it,    To Coda ⊕ — no, no,

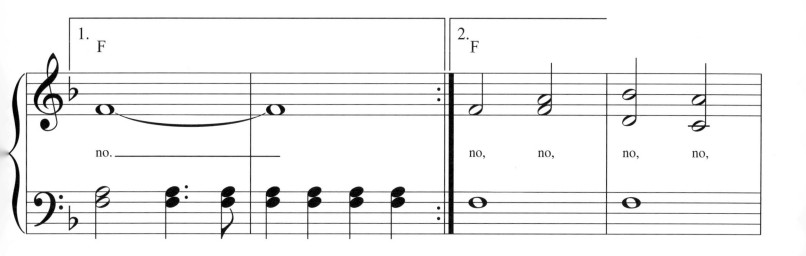

1. F — no. _____    2. F — no, no, no, no,

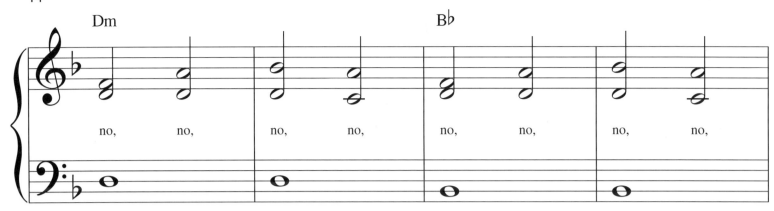

Dm                                          B♭

no,      no,        no,      no,        no,      no,        no,      no,

Csus                              C        F                              D.S. al Coda

no,      no,_____        no,      no. Chill out,    what-cha  yell-in' for?

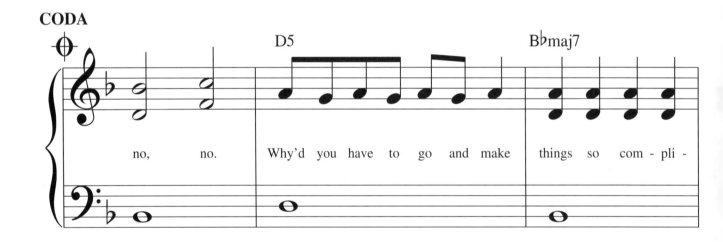

CODA

D5                              B♭maj7

no,      no.    Why'd  you  have  to  go  and  make    things  so  com-pli-

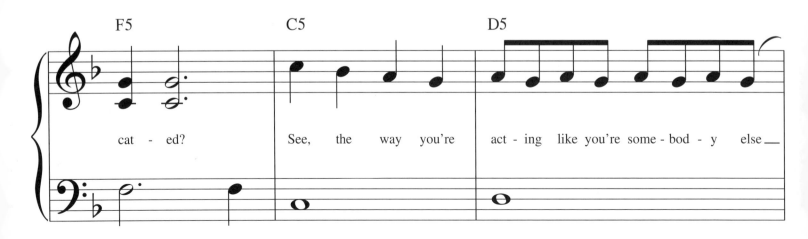

F5                              C5                    D5

cat - ed?        See,    the    way  you're    act-ing  like  you're  some-bod-y  else___

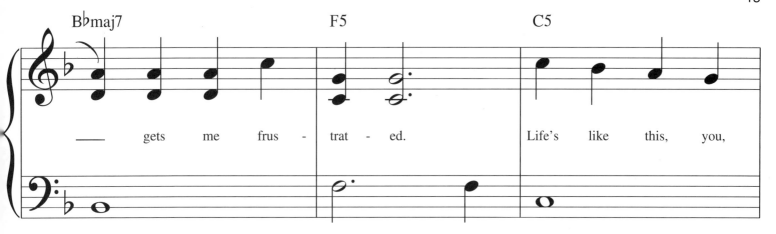

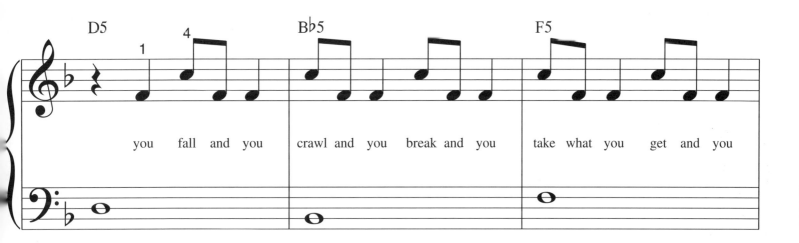

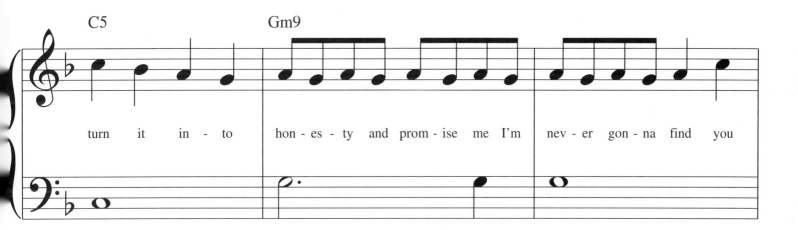

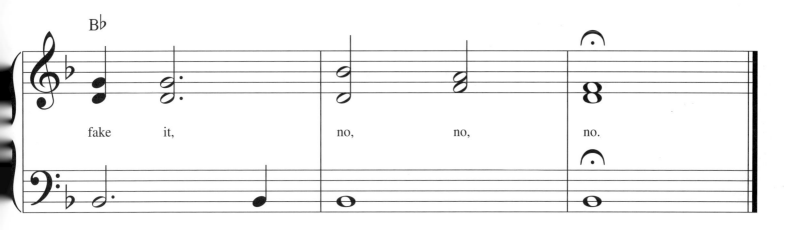

# CLOCKS

Words and Music by GUY BERRYMAN, JON BUCKLAND,
WILL CHAMPION and CHRIS MARTIN

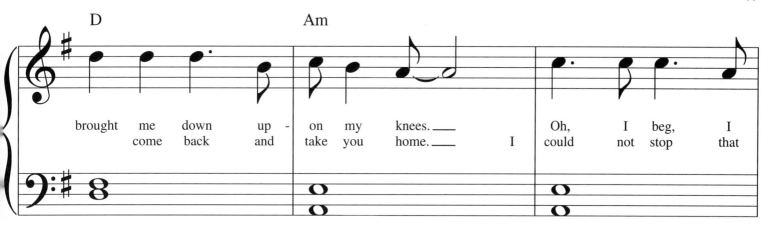

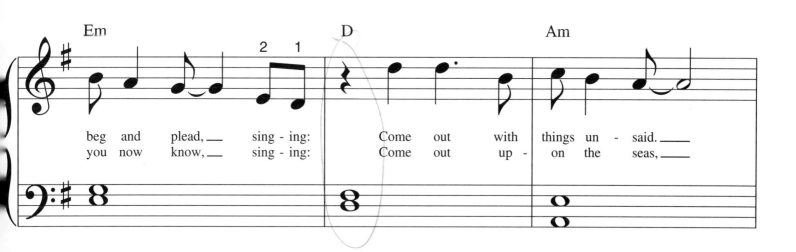

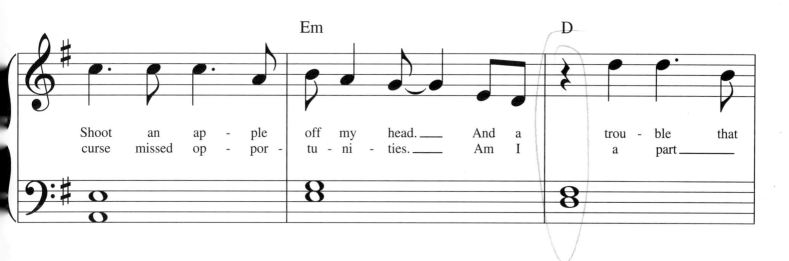

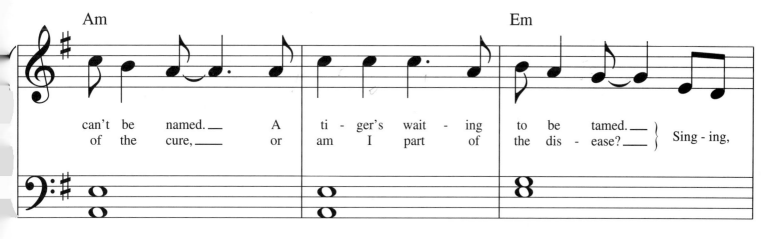

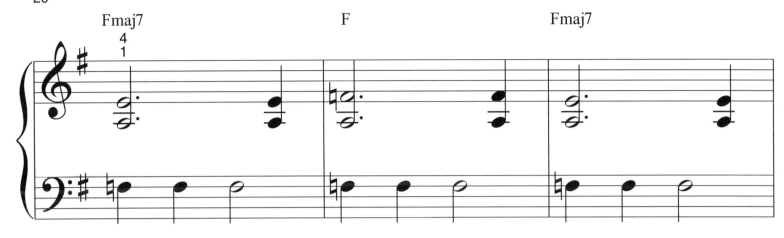

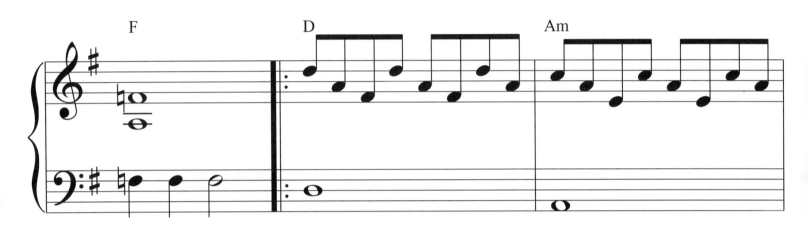

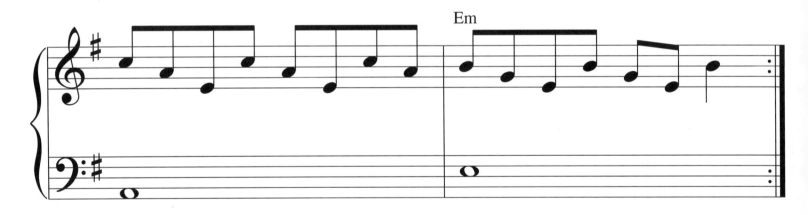

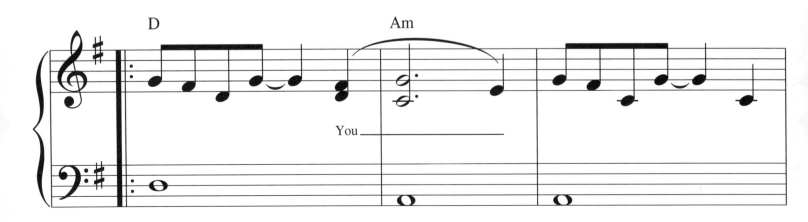

You

# DON'T KNOW WHY

Words and Music by
JESSE HARRIS

# A MOMENT LIKE THIS

Words and Music by JOHN REID
and JORGEN KJELL ELOFSSON

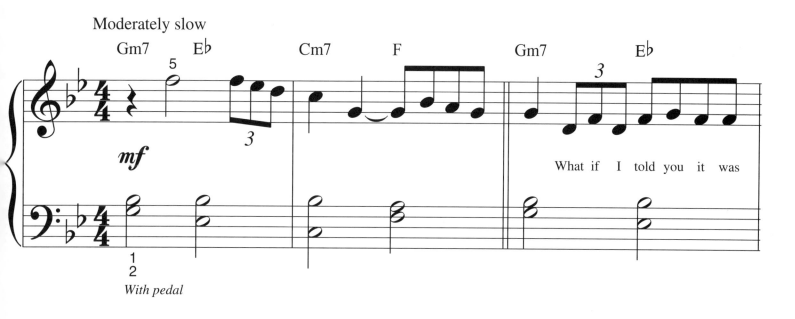

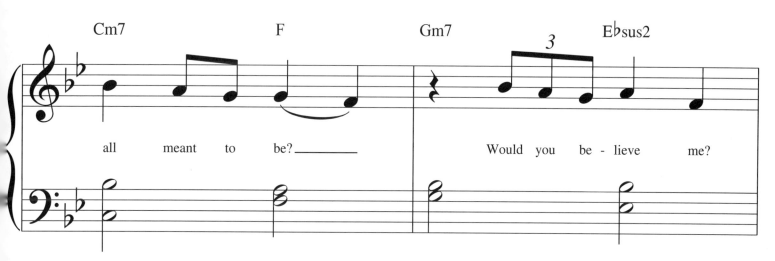

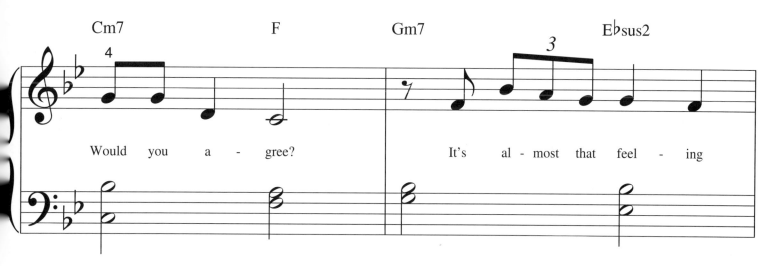

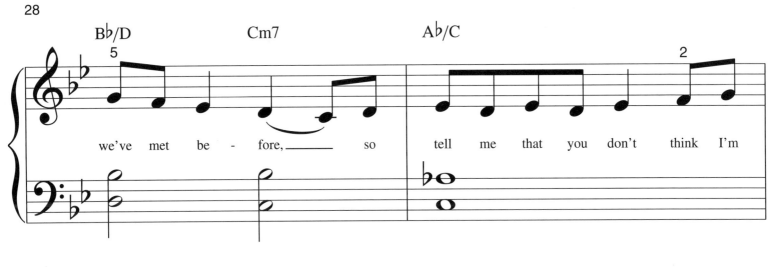

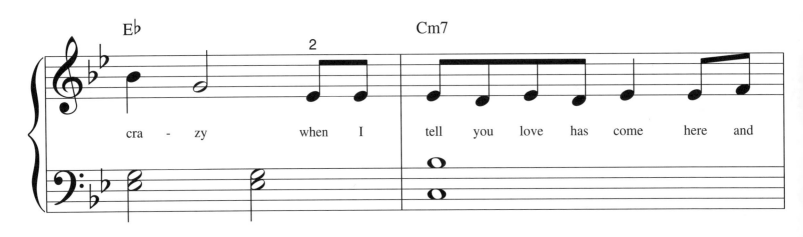

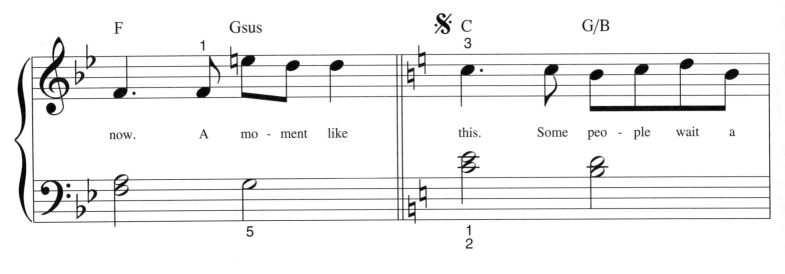

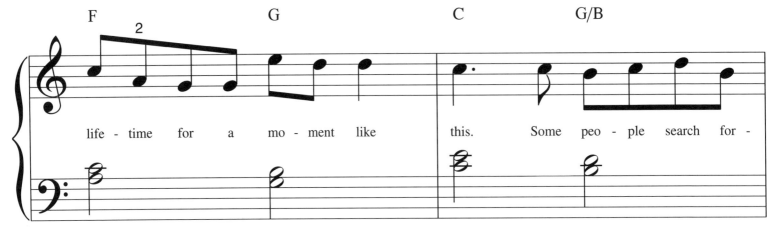

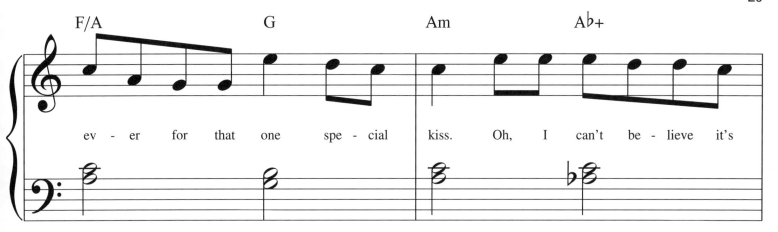

ev - er for that one spe - cial kiss. Oh, I can't be - lieve it's

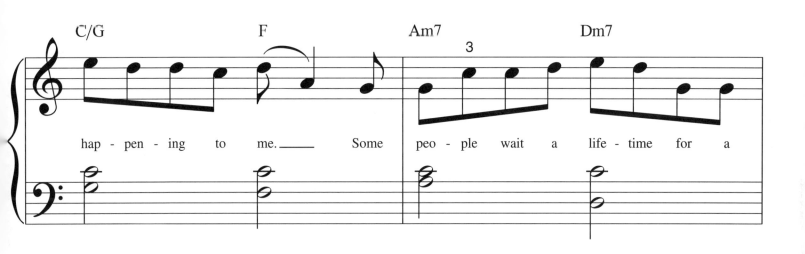

hap - pen - ing to me.____ Some peo - ple wait a life - time for a

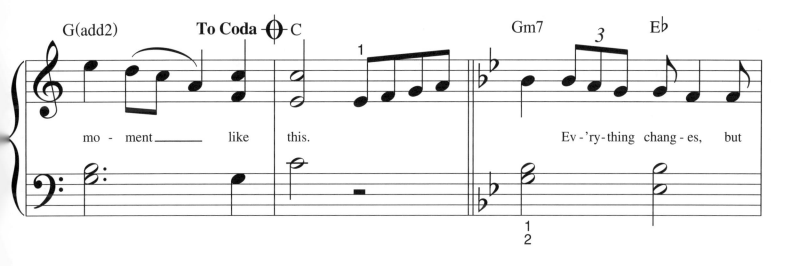

mo - ment____ like this. Ev -'ry-thing chang - es, but

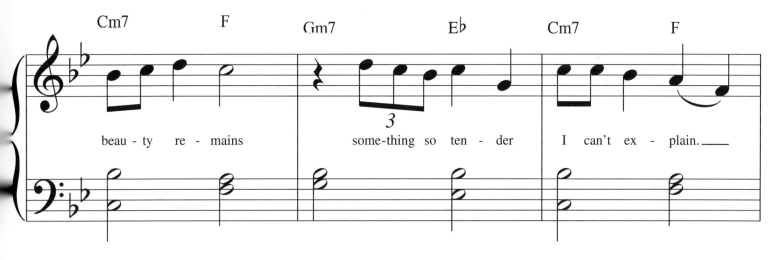

beau - ty re - mains some-thing so ten - der I can't ex - plain.____

30

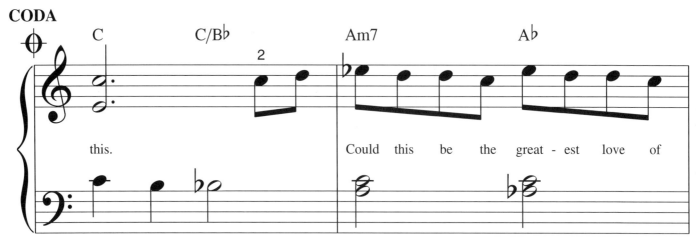

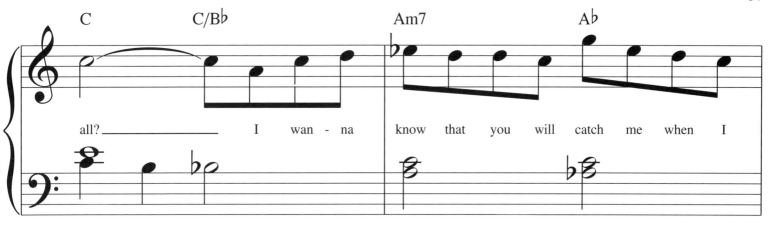

C      C/B♭      Am7      A♭

all? _____ I wan - na know that you will catch me when I

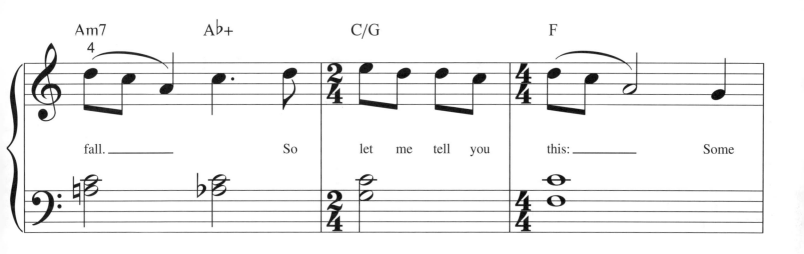

Am7      A♭+      C/G      F

fall. _____ So let me tell you this: _____ Some

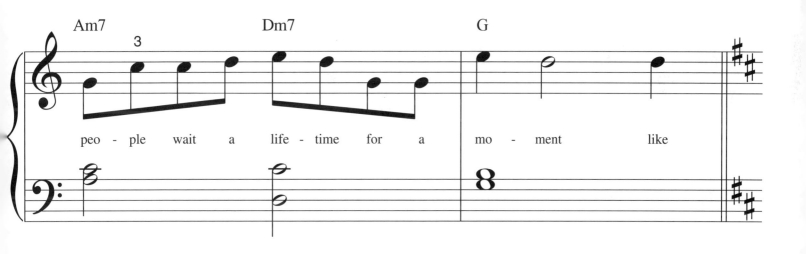

Am7      Dm7      G

peo - ple wait a life - time for a mo - ment like

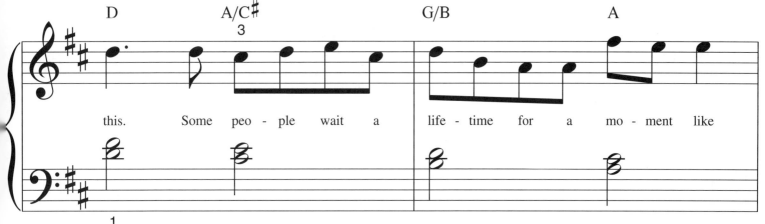

D      A/C♯      G/B      A

this. Some peo - ple wait a life - time for a mo - ment like

1
2

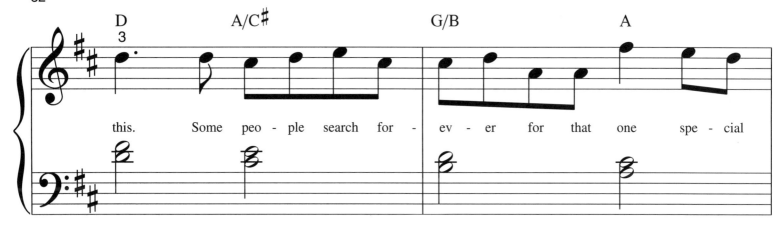

this. Some peo - ple search for - ev - er for that one spe - cial

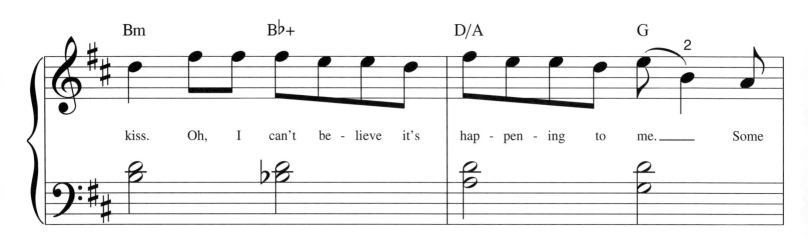

kiss. Oh, I can't be - lieve it's hap - pen - ing to me.____ Some

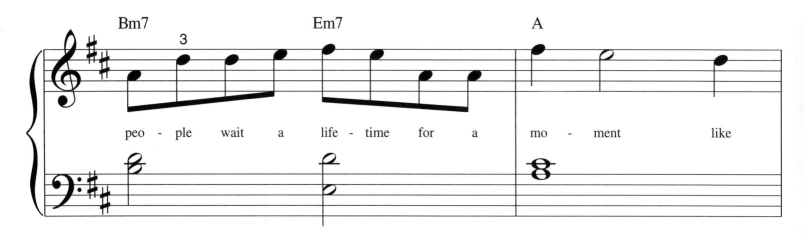

peo - ple wait a life - time for a mo - ment like

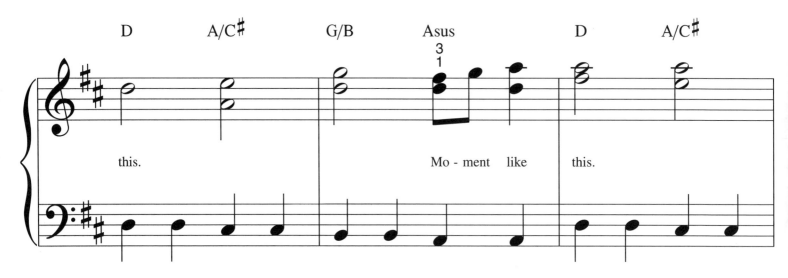

this. Mo - ment like this.

# DRIFT AWAY

Words and Music by
MENTOR WILLIAMS

36

And when my mind is free, no

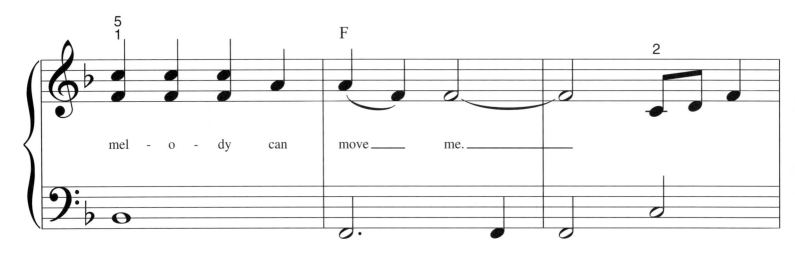

mel - o - dy can move ___ me. ___

When I'm feel - in' blue ___ gui - tars are

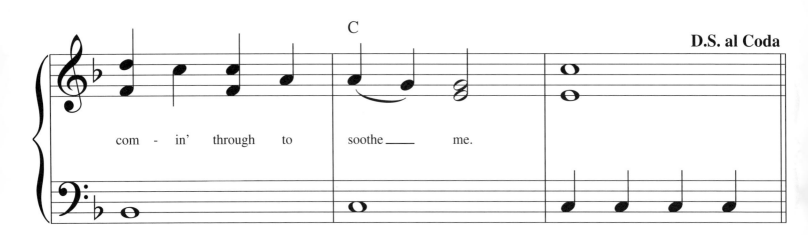

com - in' through to soothe ___ me.

**D.S. al Coda**

# FALLEN

Words and Music by
SARAH McLACHLAN

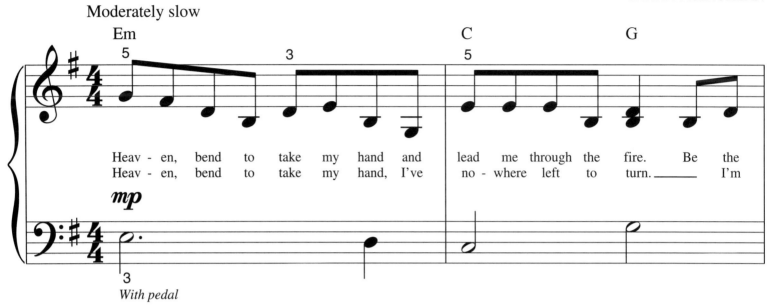

Heav - en, bend to take my hand and lead me through the fire. Be the
Heav - en, bend to take my hand, I've no - where left to turn. _____ I'm

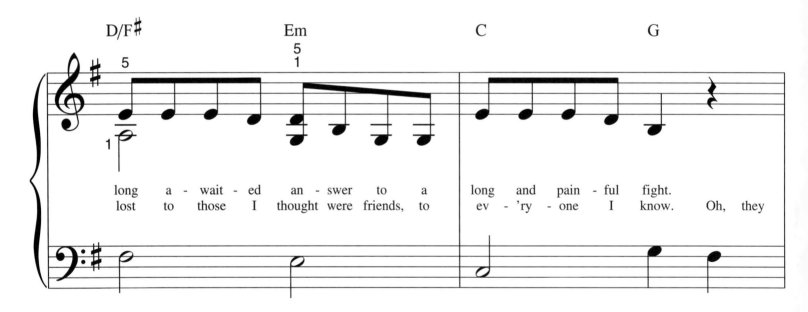

long a - wait - ed an - swer to a long and pain - ful fight.
lost to those I thought were friends, to ev - 'ry - one I know. Oh, they

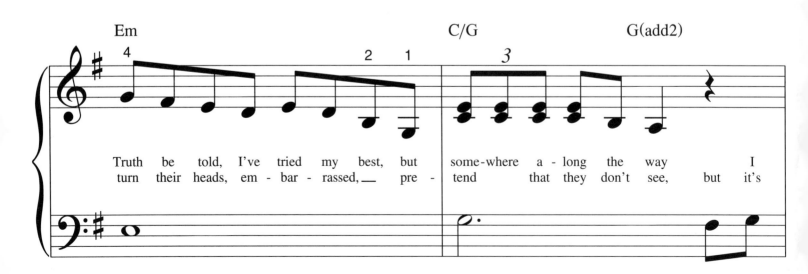

Truth be told, I've tried my best, but some - where a - long the way I
turn their heads, em - bar - rassed, ___ pre - tend that they don't see, but it's

43

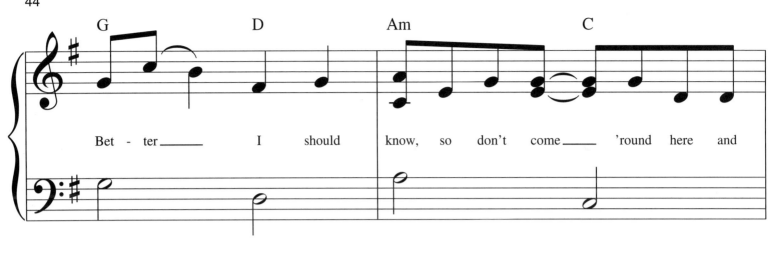

Bet - ter _____ I should know, so don't come _____ 'round here and

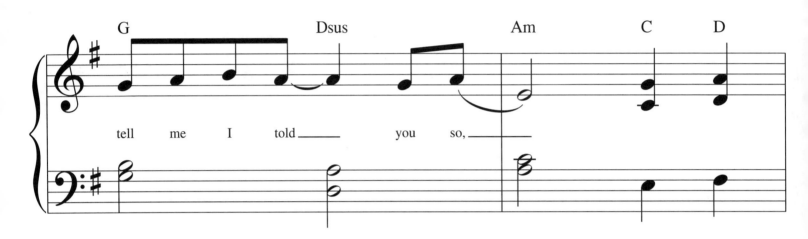

tell me I told _____ you so, _____

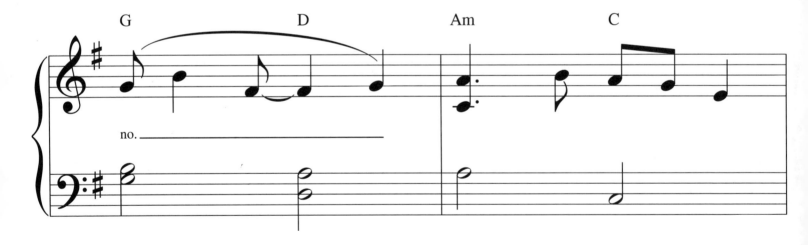

no. _____

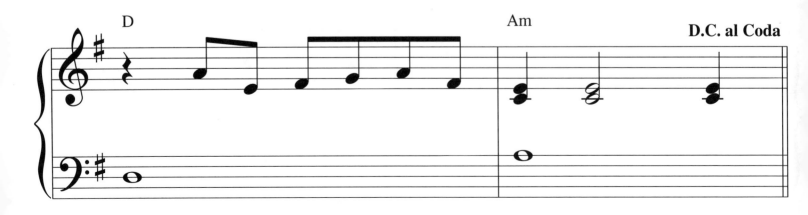

**D.C. al Coda**

# HEAVEN

Words and Music by HENRY GARZA,
JOEY GARZA and RINGO GARZA

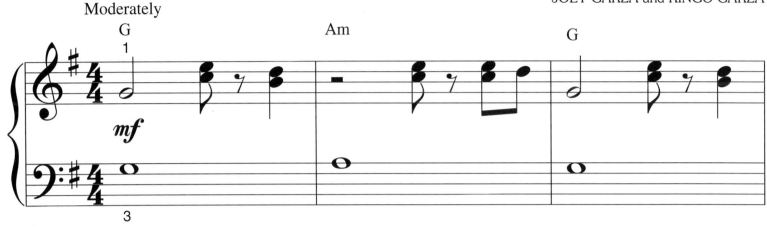

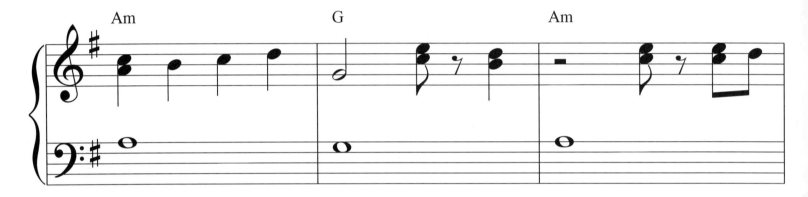

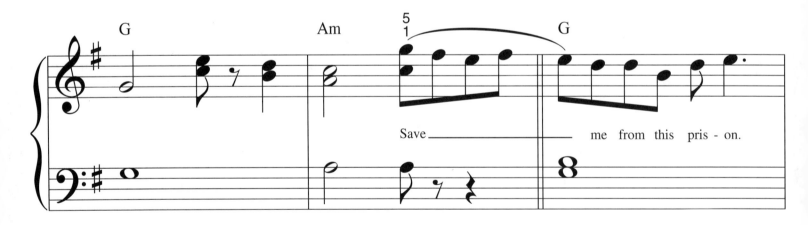

Save _____ me from this pris - on.

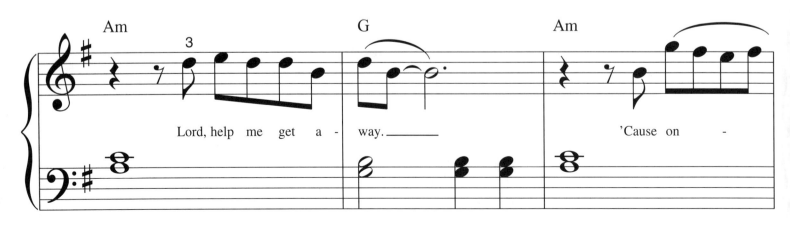

Lord, help me get a - way. _____ 'Cause on -

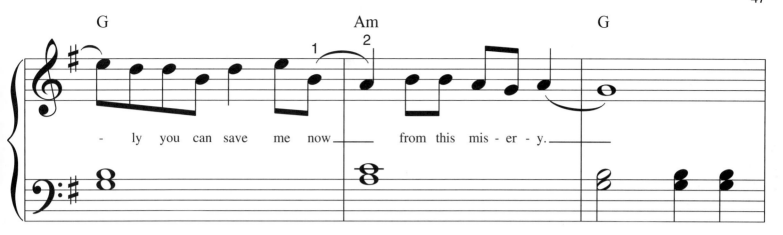

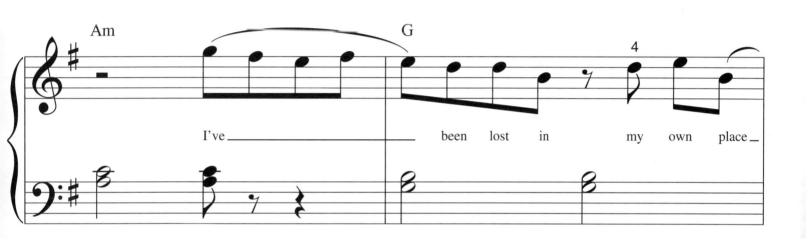

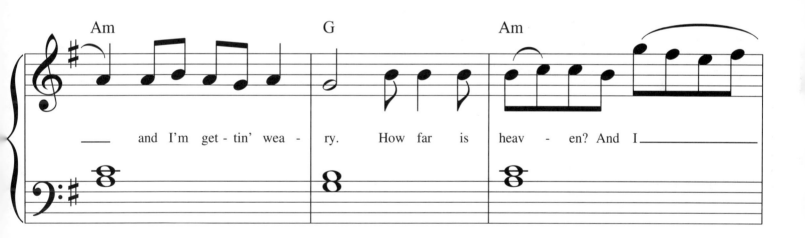

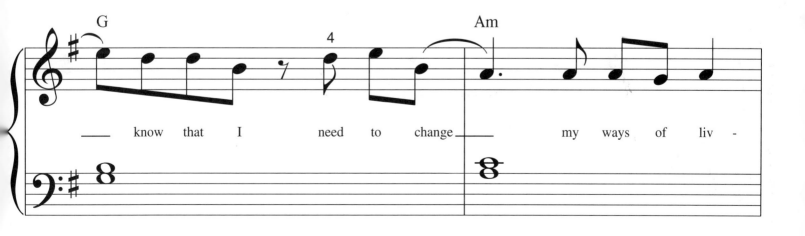

48

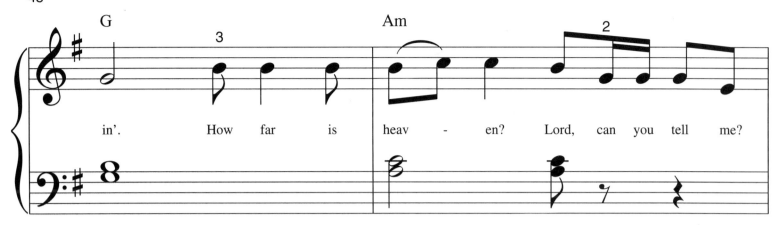

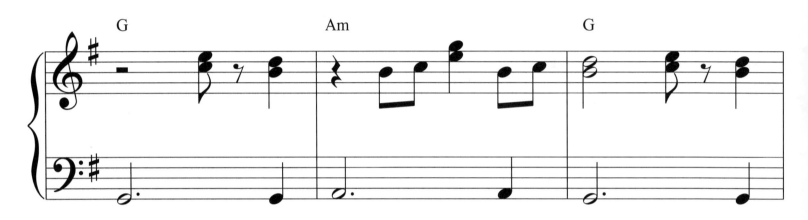

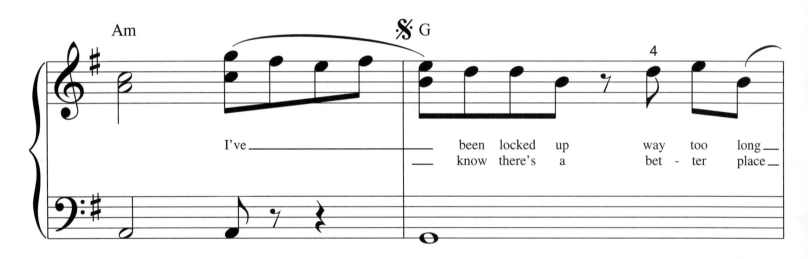

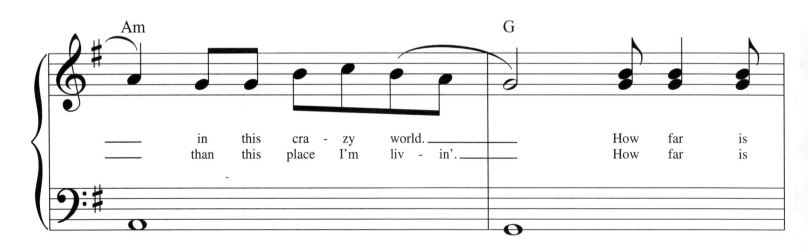

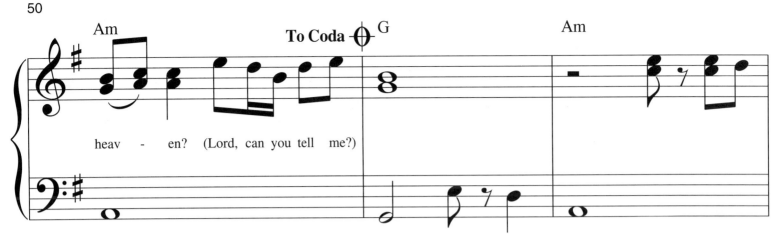

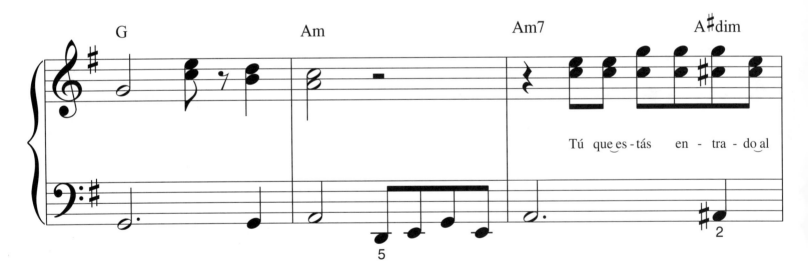

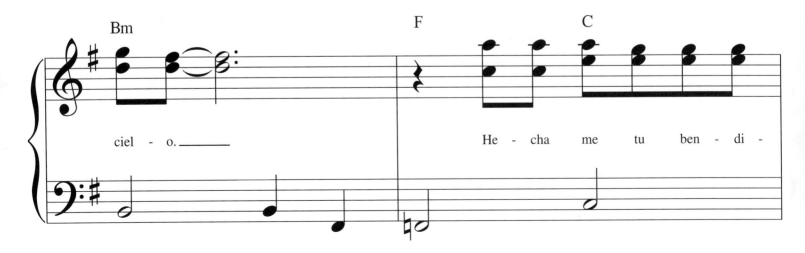

# 100 YEARS

Words and Music by
JOHN ONDRASIK

on - ly got a hun - dred years to live.

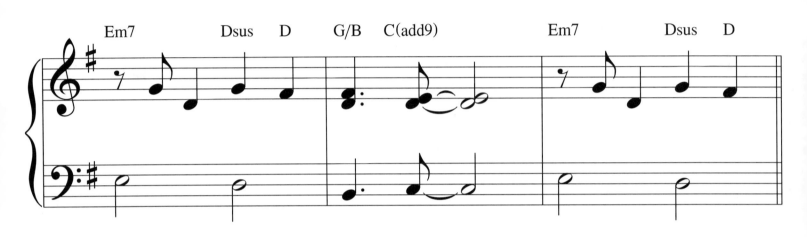

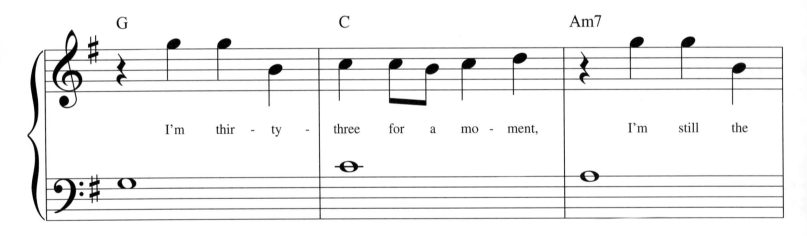

I'm thir - ty - three for a mo - ment, I'm still the

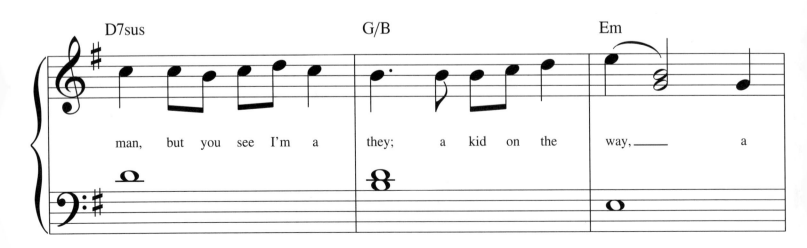

man, but you see I'm a they; a kid on the way,___ a

fam - 'ly on my mind. I'm for - ty -

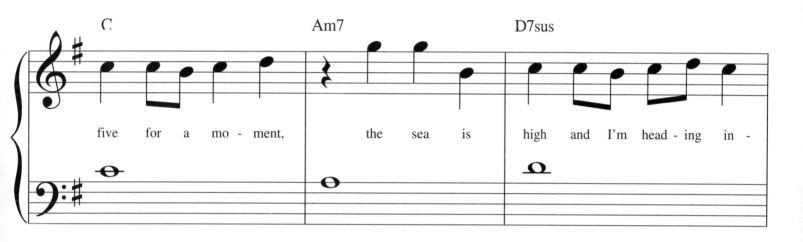

five for a mo - ment, the sea is high and I'm head - ing in -

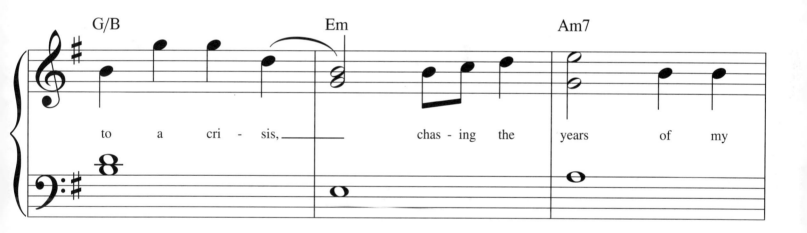

to a cri - sis, chas - ing the years of my

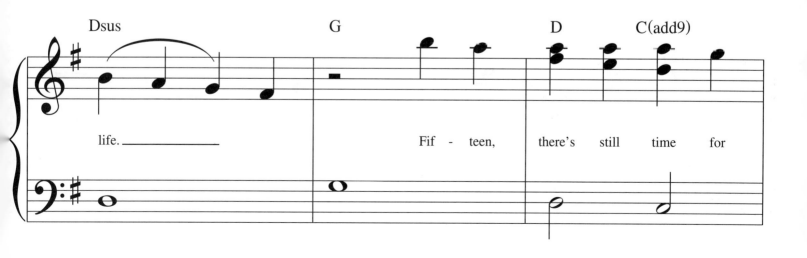

life. Fif - teen, there's still time for

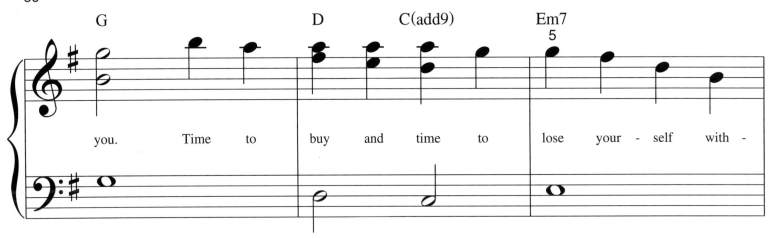

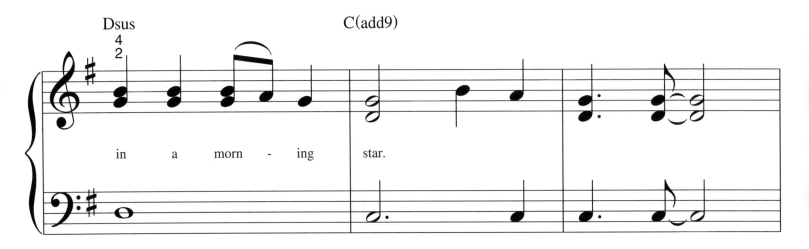

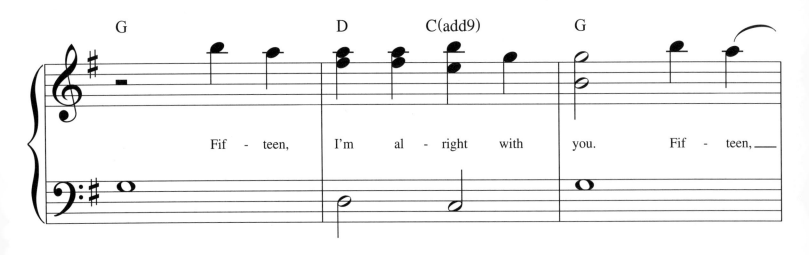

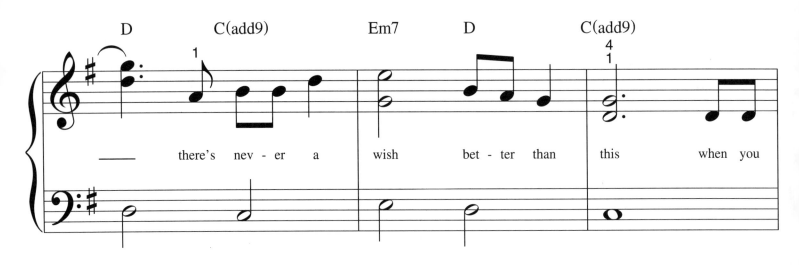

on - ly got a hun - dred years to live. Half time goes

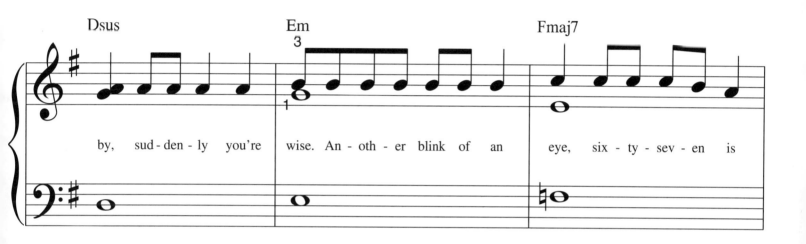

by, sud - den - ly you're wise. An - oth - er blink of an eye, six - ty - sev - en is

gone. The sun is get - ting high, we're mov - ing on...

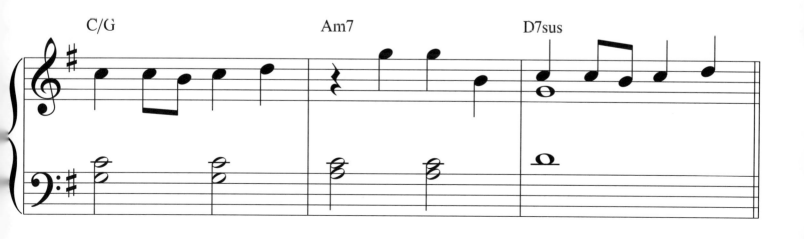

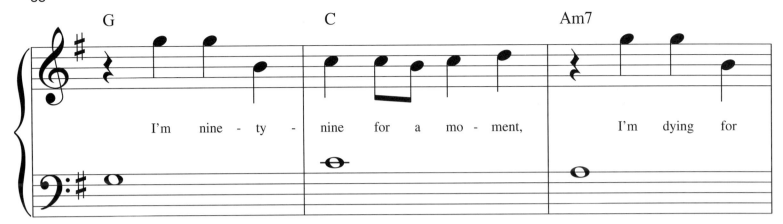

I'm nine-ty-nine for a mo-ment, I'm dying for

just an-oth-er mo-ment and I'm just dream-ing,_____ count-ing the

ways to where you are._____ Fif - teen,

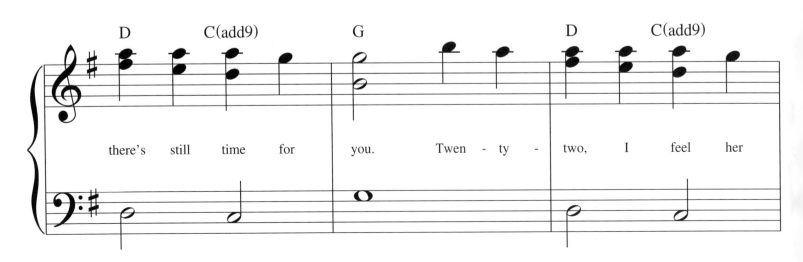

there's still time for you. Twen-ty-two, I feel her

60

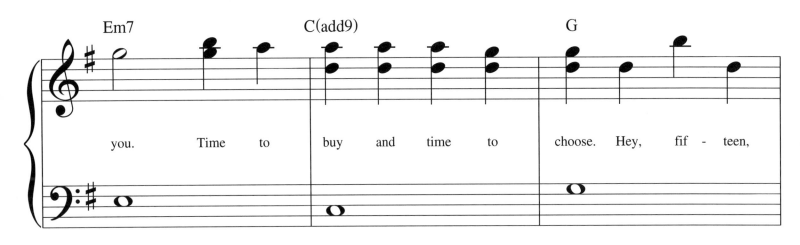

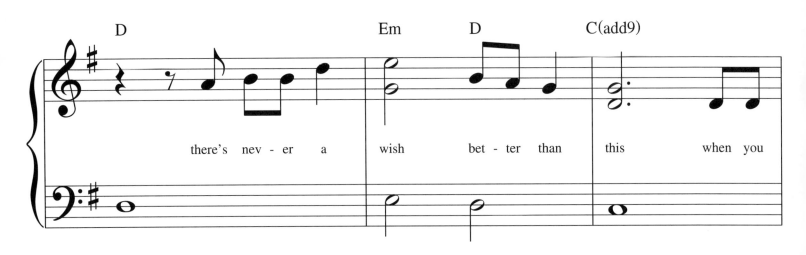

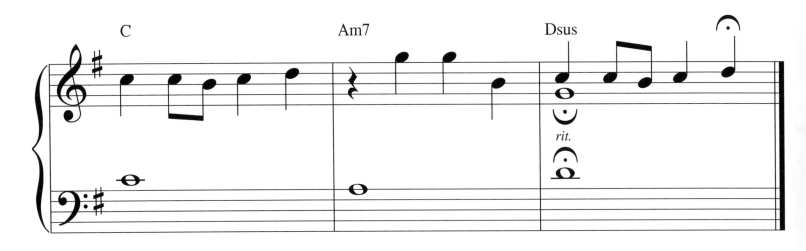

# SHE WILL BE LOVED

Words and Music by ADAM LEVINE
and JAMES VALENTINE

64

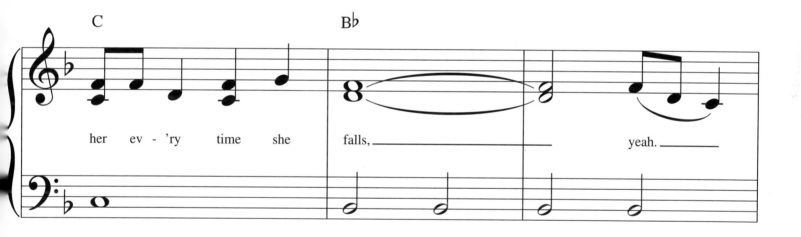

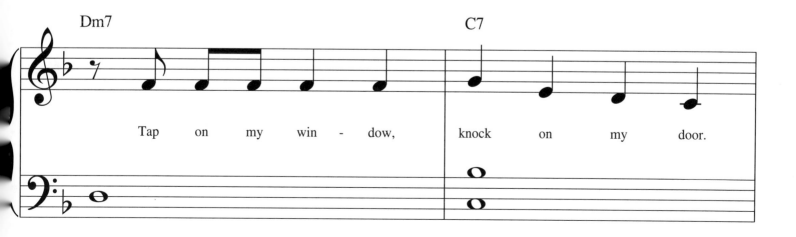

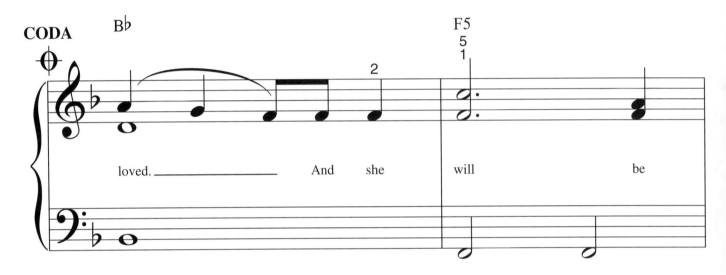

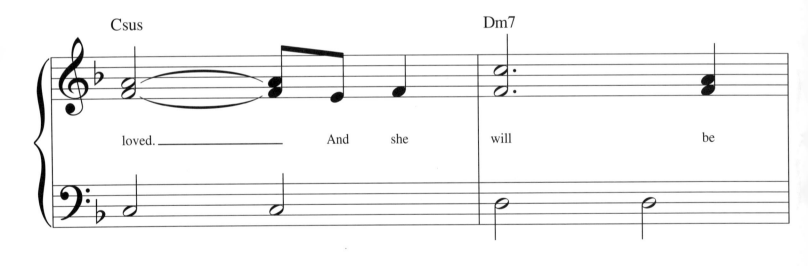

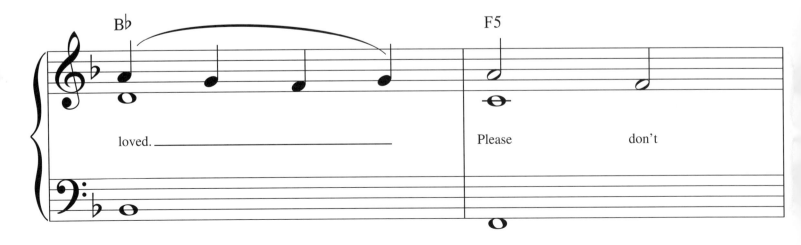

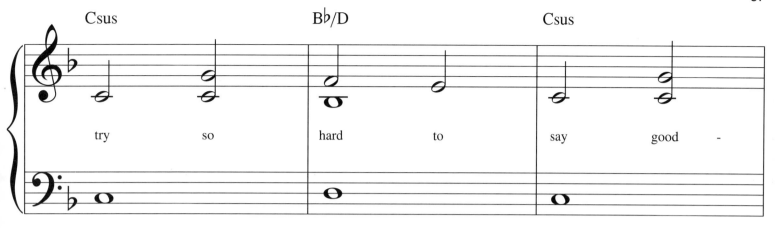

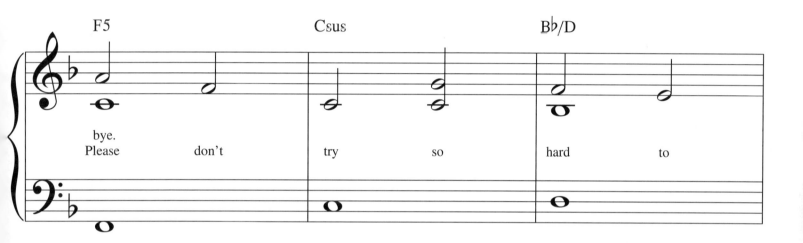

# PIECES OF ME

Words and Music by ASHLEE SIMPSON,
JOHN SHANKS and KARA DioGUARDI

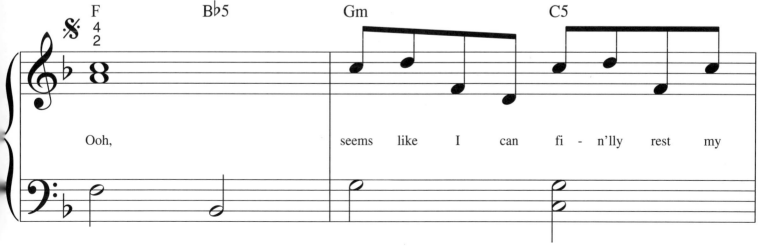

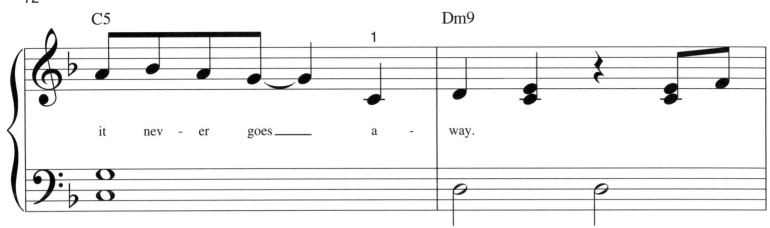

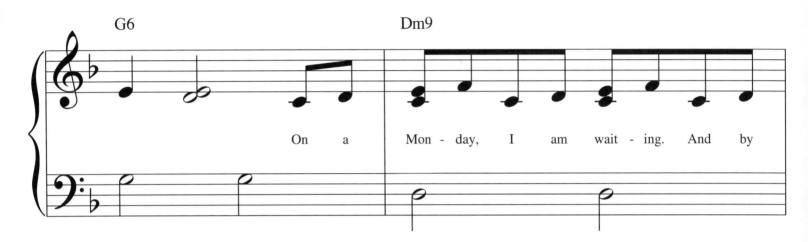

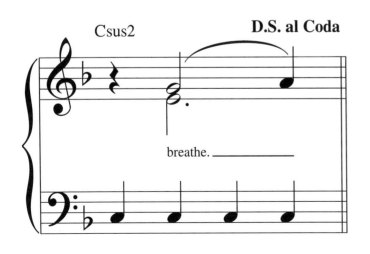

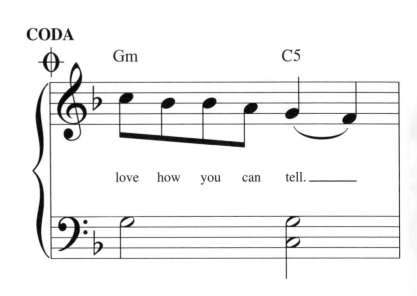

# A THOUSAND MILES

Words and Music by
VANESSA CARLTON

1., 3. Mak - ing my way down -
2. *(See additional lyrics)*

town, walk - ing fast, fac - es pass and I'm home - bound.

**Chorus**

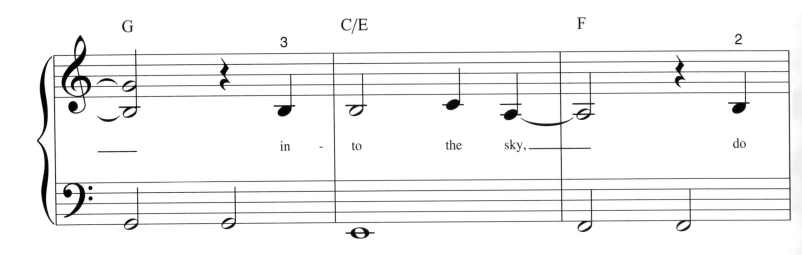

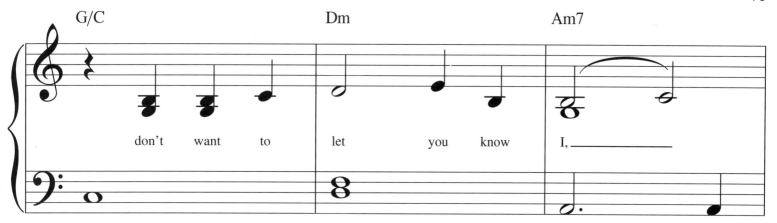

G/C                         Dm                        Am7

don't want to        let you know        I, _____

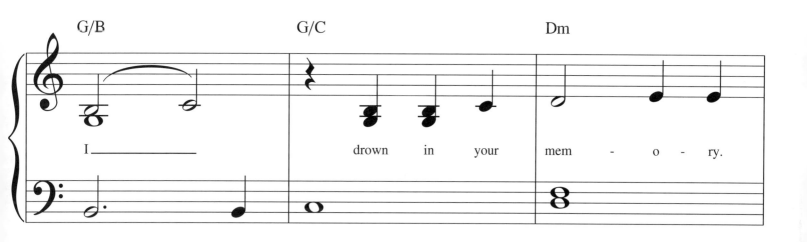

G/B                         G/C                        Dm

I _____        drown in your        mem - o - ry.

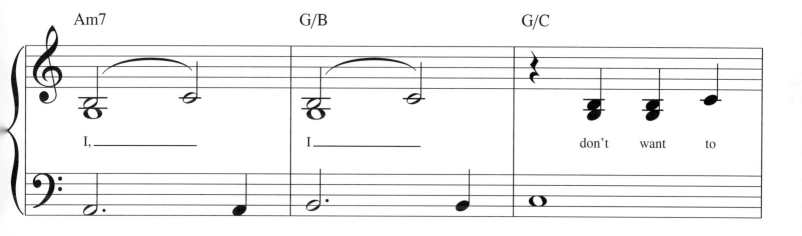

Am7                       G/B                        G/C

I, _____      I _____      don't want to

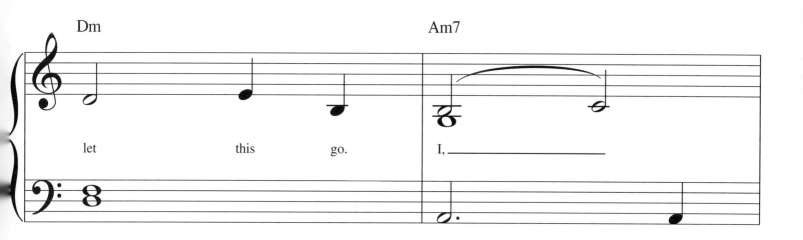

Dm                                 Am7

let this go.         I, _____

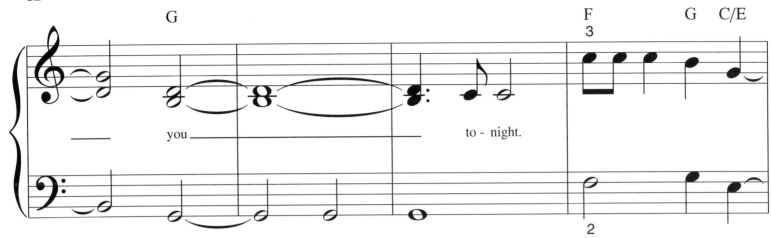

you _____ to - night.

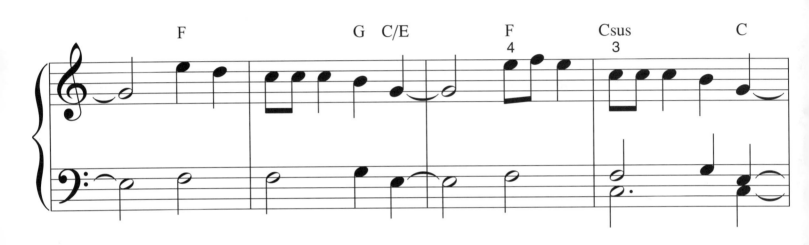

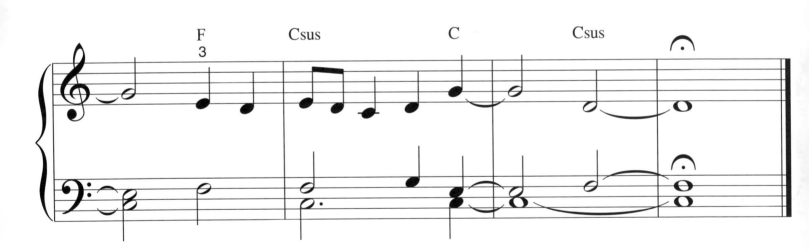

*Additional Lyrics*

2. It's always times like these when I think of you
And wonder if you ever think of me.
'Cause everything's so wrong and I don't belong
Living in your precious memory.
'Cause I need you,
and I'll miss you,
And I wonder...
*Chorus*

# YOU DON'T KNOW MY NAME

Words and Music by ALICIA KEYS, KANYE OMARI WEST,
HAROLD SPENCER LILLY, J.R. BAILEY,
MEL KENT and KEN WILLIAMS

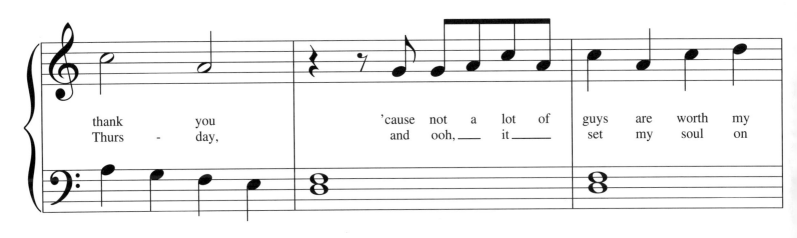

thank        you
Thurs  -  day,

'cause  not  a  lot  of
and  ooh,___  it___

guys   are   worth   my
set   my   soul   on

E7

Dm7

time._____
fire._____

Ooh,___      ba - by,  ba - by,
Ooh,___      ba - by,  ba - by,

ba  -  by,
ba  -  by,

it's  get - tin'  kind - a
I   can't  wait  for  the

cra  -  zy,_____
first   time._____

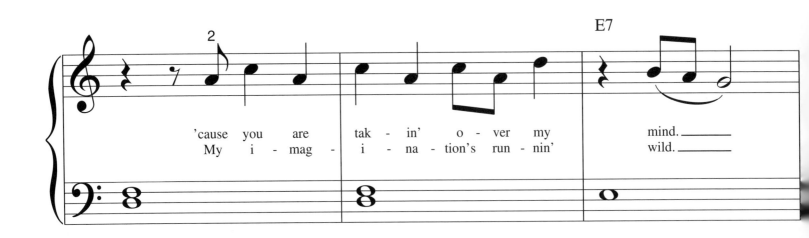

'cause   you   are
My   i - mag -

tak - in'   o - ver   my
i - na - tion's  run - nin'

E7

mind._____
wild._____

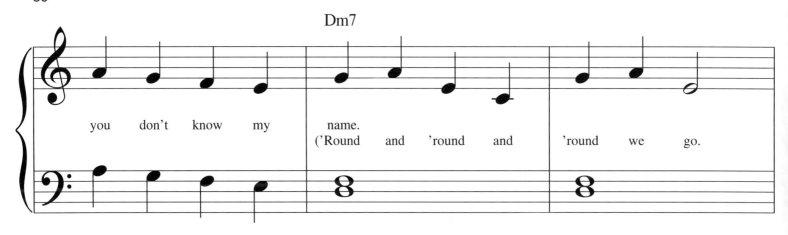

Dm7

you don't know my name.
('Round and 'round and 'round we go.

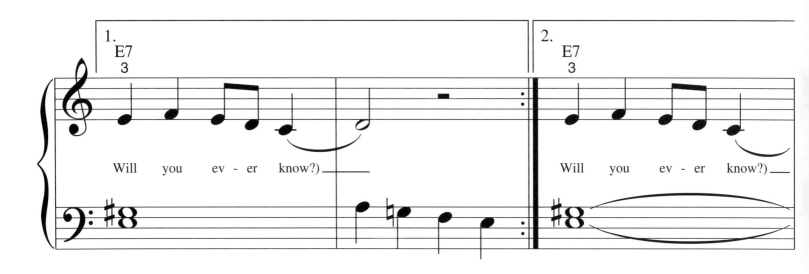

1.
E7
Will you ev - er know?)

2.
E7
Will you ev - er know?)

Cmaj7

*Spoken: I'm sayin'...*

*He don't*

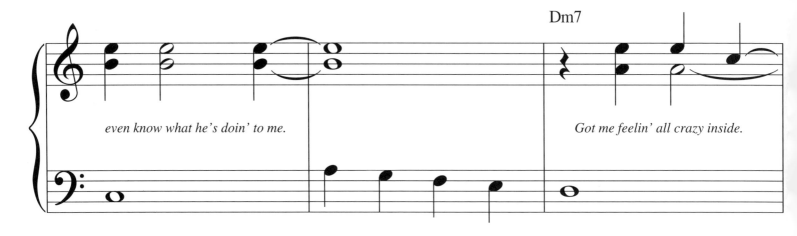

*even know what he's doin' to me.*

Dm7

*Got me feelin' all crazy inside.*

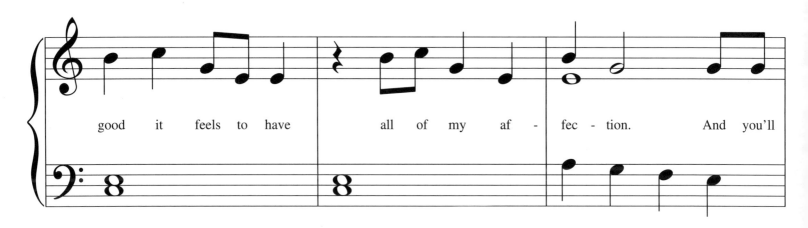

good it feels to have all of my af - fec - tion. And you'll

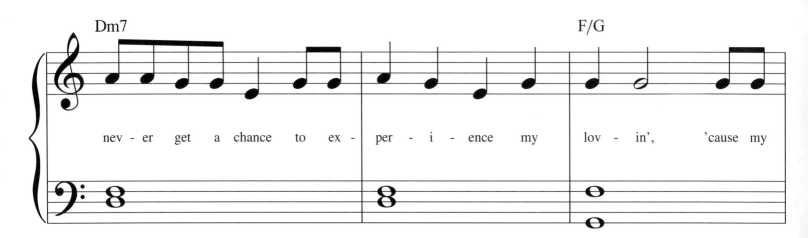

Dm7
F/G

nev - er get a chance to ex - per - i - ence my lov - in', 'cause my

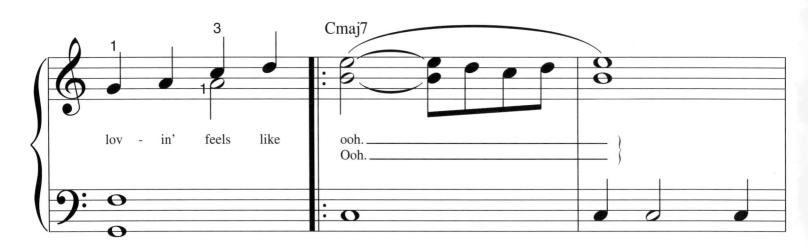

Cmaj7

lov - in' feels like ooh._____
Ooh._____

Dm7

You don't know my name.
('Round and 'round and

Will you ev - er know it?

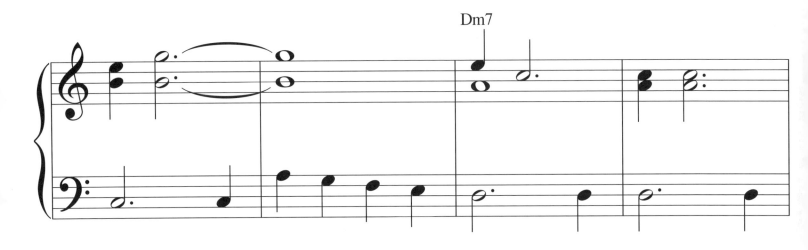

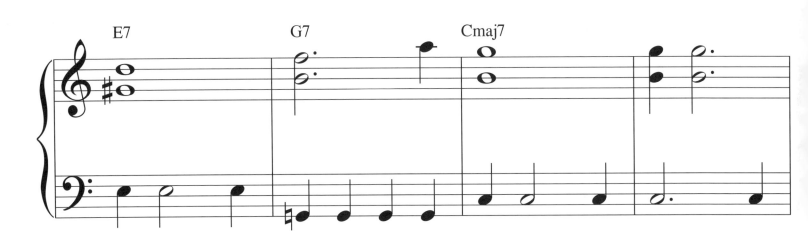

# YOU RAISE ME UP

Words and Music by BRENDAN GRAHAM
and ROLF LOVLAND

When I am down and oh, my soul's so wea - ry, when trou - bles

come and my heart bur - dened be, then I am still and wait here in the

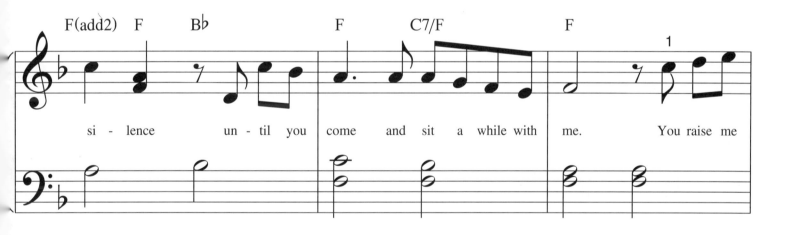

si - lence un - til you come and sit a while with me. You raise me

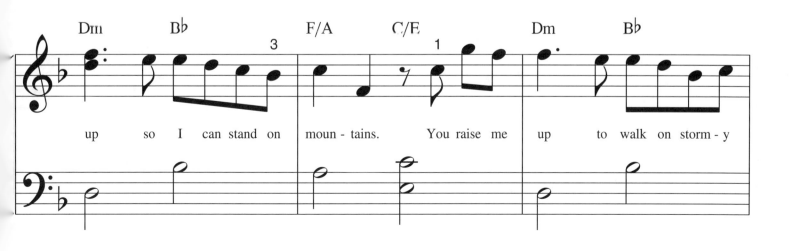

up so I can stand on moun - tains. You raise me up to walk on storm - y

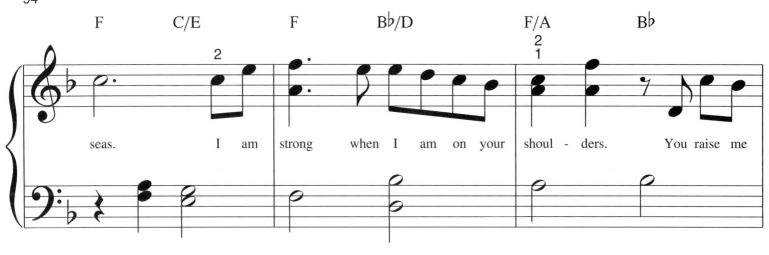

seas.          I am strong    when I am on your  shoul - ders.          You raise me

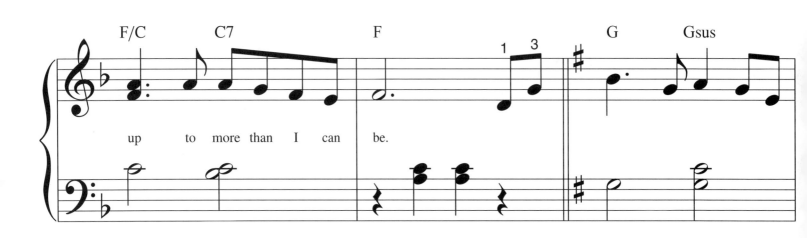

up      to more than  I  can     be.

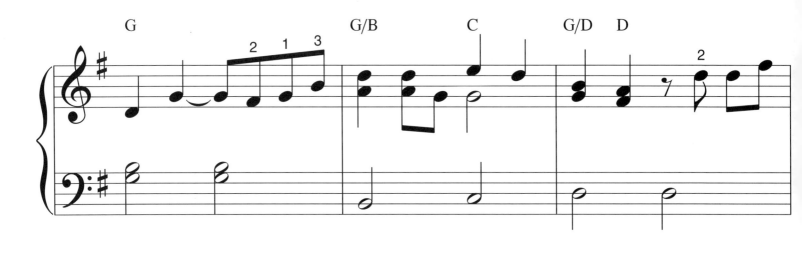

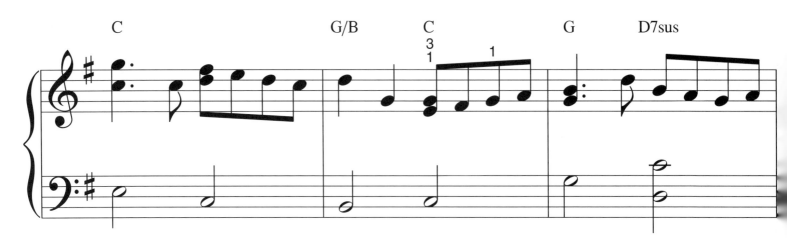